Lights! Camera! Celebrate!

Lights!
Camera!
Celebrate!

HOLLYWOOD BIRTHDAYS, BASHES AND BLOWOUTS

by David Marsh

Design by John Miller and Dan Nadeau

ANGEL CITY PRESS

SANTA MONICA

ANGEL CITY PRESS, INC.

Published by Angel City Press

2118 Wilshire Boulevard, Suite 880; Santa Monica, California 90403; 310-395-9982

First published in 1995 by Angel City Press

1 3 5 7 9 10 8 6 4 2

FIRST EDITION

Text copyright 1995 by David Marsh

ISBN 1-883318-26-2

Art design: John Miller and Dan Nadeau

LIBRARY OF CONGRESS CATALOGING-IN-PUBLICATION DATA

Lights! camera! celebrate! : Hollywood birthdays, bashes, and blowouts/compiled by David Marsh; design by John Miller and Dan Nadeau.—1st ed.

p.   cm.

ISBN 1-883318-26-2

1. Motion picture actors and actresses—California—Los Angeles—Anniversaries, etc.—Pictorial works. I. Marsh, David, 1950 Oct. 25-

PN1998.2.L54   1995   95-32223

791.43'028'092279494—dc20   CIP

Printed in the United States of America

Frontispiece: **Leave Her to Heaven** (20th Century-Fox, 1945)
Jeanne Crain contemplates her 20th birthday.

Above: **Carefree** (RKO, 1938)
Ginger Rogers celebrates her 27th birthday, with choreographer Hermes Pan (far left), Fred Astaire, and director Mark Sandrich (next to Astaire).

Opposite: **Two Girls on Broadway**
(Metro-Goldwyn-Mayer, 1940) Lana Turner turns 20, flanked by director S. Sylvan Simon and future California senator George Murphy.

THE SWEATER
GIRL, FROM THE
GANG THAT MADE
THE YARN

Introduction

From its earliest days, one of the staples of the studio publicity mill was a still photograph of a spontaneously staged celebration. During a break in filming, the cast (in costume) would gather around the obligatory cake to note a birthday, an anniversary or any other occasion that provided an excuse to celebrate. The resulting photo might appear in a newspaper or, more likely, a movie magazine.

It was a minor thing, just one of hundreds of stills taken during the course of production. But the celebration had a special significance, nonetheless: it was a "just folks" moment, geared to bring the stars down from their lofty pedestals (for a moment, anyway) and show that they were just like you and me. After all, who hasn't had their picture taken, surrounded by friends and family, as they blew out the candles?

Indeed, what's intriguing about these photographs is the number of striking dichotomies. They are obviously staged and artificial, yet a sweetness and spontaneity comes through, taking them out of the realm of the stiff movie star portrait. It also becomes clear, if one looks closely, that a movie star wears the costume, but it is a person who inhabits it. While all stars were required to pose for these kinds of photographs, some, like Joan Crawford (page 3) reveled in it. Look at her eye-popping, animated, center-of-attention demeanor (although no one seems to be paying her much attention) in contrast to Bette Davis (page 12) with her resigned slouch and wan smile. Compare Nelson Eddy's tight-lipped peevishness at co-star

Jeanette MacDonald's celebration (page 10) as if he is wondering if his birthday the following week will receive as much attention — to Fred Astaire's tolerant amusement of dance partner Ginger Rogers's antic behavior on the set of *Carefree*. And look at the crew, the unsung, and usually unphotographed faces of the behind-the-scenes people who made the movies. Their raucous enjoyment often contrasts sharply with the more genteel deportment of the stars.

The tension in the off-camera shots often makes them the most fascinating, though they were only a part of the total publicity package. Studios generated still books for all their film titles. Volumes of photographs were taken during the making of a movie and used around the world for publicity purposes. Scene stills (photographs taken of the action while cameras were rolling) gave a sense of the film's story. Gallery portraits focused on the star's image. But photos of the off-camera moments of the cast, whether genuine or staged candid moments, were meant to project the human interest side of film-making: stars huddled in conversation with their directors, cast members clowning for the camera or just relaxing between shots.

Gallery portraits were taken by name photographers (Hurrell, Clarence Sinclair Bull, Ruth Harriet Louise), but scene stills and off-camera stills were taken by anonymous set photographers. They were necessary craftspeople, cogs in a wheel, no more exalted than the electrician, the wardrobe mistress, the lighting technician. They were not seen as the artists they were; they did not own the rights to their work. They had a job to do and they performed it. Ironically, many of the images that have burned themselves into our collective Hollywood unconscious were taken by photographers who never received individual credit.

Tastes have changed. Today, a movie star with a cake is not as interesting to the general public as a movie star photographed in an awkward, embarrassing situation on the cover of a tabloid. And, with the collapse of the studio system, the process of making movies changed. Actors could make their own professional and personal decisions. Studio public relations departments no longer dictated the image that a "movie star" must project.

Many of the photographs in this book have never been published. They have never been gathered in one volume. They are meant to be enjoyed.

Like a celebration.

— *David Marsh*

Preceding pages: **How Could You, Jean?** (Paramount-Artcraft, 1918)
By 1918, Mary Pickford's appeal was international. The year before they joined forces to create United Artists Corporation, Douglas Fairbanks, Mary Pickford, and Charlie Chaplin visit Miss Pickford's set and pose with a cake sent to "The Girl Who Has Won Australia's Heart" from a fan in Sydney, Australia.

Opposite: **The Gorgeous Hussy** (Metro-Goldwyn-Mayer, 1936)
Fastidious Joan Crawford was too busy filming to host a proper party for her friend, P.R. man Jerry Asher, so she invited him to the set and threw him one there. Naturally, she made sure there was a camera nearby to record her generosity.

Following pages: **Lady of the Pavements** (United Artists, 1929)
Director D.W. Griffith (straw hat), tweaks the ear of character actor George Fawcett as cast and crew assemble to commemorate Fawcett's 68th birthday. Joining the festivities are Albert Conti (behind bouquet), Lupe Velez (leaning on Fawcett's arm), William "Hopalong Cassidy" Boyd (behind Velez), Fawcett, Griffith, Jetta Goudal (in tiara), and cinematographer Karl Struss (in glasses). Griffith would direct only two more films.

Preceding pages: **Smilin' Through** (Metro-Goldwyn-Mayer, 1932)
Armed with a sabre, Norma Shearer is poised to cut into her 32nd birthday cake. Joining her are screenwriter Donald Ogden Stewart, co-star Fredric March (in costume for his subsequent film *The Sign of the Cross*), sister Athole (Mrs. Howard) Hawks, husband Irving Thalberg, director Sidney Franklin, Albert Lewin, and leading man Leslie Howard (in age makeup).

Opposite: **The Woman Accused** (Paramount, 1933)
Hollywood's most famous bachelor housemates, Randoph Scott and Cary Grant, share their 30th and 29th birthdays with Nancy Carroll, Grant's co-star in *The Woman Accused*.

Following pages, clockwise from top left:
Sweethearts (Metro-Goldwyn-Mayer, 1938)
Filming had just begun when Jeanette MacDonald was honored with a party celebrating her 37th birthday. Co-star Nelson Eddy (looking a little peevish) joins director W. S. Van Dyke and MGM executive Eddie Mannix in congratulating the warbling soprano star.

Go West Young Man (Paramount, 1936)
As filming got underway on her seventh film, Mae West was the highest paid woman in the United States. Here she hosts a birthday party for Emanuel Cohen, president of Major Pictures, the company formed to distribute Miss West's films. Joining them are director Henry Hathaway, Major Pictures' vice-president Ben Piazza, and co-star Warren Williams.

Spawn of the North (Paramount, 1938)
By the time he made his 13th film, Henry Fonda's quintessentially "American" screen persona was firmly established. At his 30th birthday party, he looks as if he's going to lop off the frosting-filching finger of co-star Louise Platt.

More than a Secretary (Columbia, 1936)
On the set of her 66th film, husky-voiced comedienne extraordinaire Jean Arthur celebrates her 31st birthday with co-stars Dorothea Kent, Lionel Stander, and Ruth Donnelly. Miss Arthur would reach her peak in popularity in Frank Capra's social comedies a few years later.

Above: **Of Human Bondage** (RKO, 1934)
Bette Davis fought for the opportunity to portray Mildred, W. Somerset Maugham's snide, selfish Cockney waitress, and established her reputation as an uncompromising, first-rate actress. Here she celebrates her 26th birthday with co-star Leslie Howard, celebrating his 41st.

Opposite: **Wuthering Heights** (United Artists — Goldwyn, 1939)
Although Laurence Olivier wanted girlfriend Vivien Leigh to play the role of Cathy, Samuel Goldwyn was adamant the part go to Merle Oberon. On the set of her final film for Goldwyn, Miss Oberon is feted with a party for her 28th birthday. Joining her is David Niven, along with property master Irving Sindler, who manages to push himself front and center.

Following pages: **Sylvia Scarlett** (RKO, 1935)
Not only was George Cukor's film RKO's worst financial failure of the year, it was condemned by the Legion of Decency, and set in motion Katharine Hepburn's descent into being branded "box office poison." In happier times, Miss Hepburn and co-star Brian Aherne serve birthday boy Edmund Gwenn a slice of cake at the on-set party marking his 60th year.

Above: **Zaza** (Paramount, 1939)
Director George Cukor accepts the first piece of leading lady Claudette Colbert's 33rd birthday cake.

Right: **The Women** (Metro-Goldwyn-Mayer, 1939)
By 1939, Cukor had gained so much weight that his 40th birthday, which fell on the final day of filming, was observed with watermelon. Battling co-stars Joan Crawford and Norma Shearer join the crew in wishing the dieting director a happy day.

Preceding pages: **The Bride Comes Home** (Paramount, 1935)
Having won the Oscar for *It Happened One Night* earlier that year, Claudette Colbert's luck seemed in good shape. Her 30th birthday, which fell on Friday the 13th, was awash with black cats just in case. She is joined by director Wesley Ruggles (left) and her mother, Jeanne (striped scarf).

Opposite: **Top Hat** (RKO, 1935)
During the filming of the dance number "Cheek to Cheek," several of the feathers from Ginger Rogers's gown became airborne and dance partner Fred Astaire had to avoid inhaling them. Here, Miss Rogers presents her hairdresser, Louise Sloan, with a coconut-topped birthday cake, undoubtedly much easier to swallow.

Following pages: **Lost Horizon** (Columbia, 1937)
Director Frank Capra's 39th birthday cake was a re-creation of art director Stephen Goosson's Academy Award-winning set for Shangri-La. Joining Capra are Ronald Colman, Jane Wyatt, Isabel Jewell, and H. B. Warner.

Above: **Nothing but the Truth** (Paramount, 1941)
On the set of their third screen pairing, Bob Hope's 38th birthday fell in the same week as Paulette Goddard's 30th, so the crew congratulated the couple with a communal cake.

Opposite: **Little Miss Broadway** (20th Century-Fox, 1938)
Shirley Temple warns her penguin co-star to have a happy birthday

Preceding pages, clockwise from top left: **The Lady is Willing** (Columbia, 1942)
Assistant director Francisco "Chico" Day (the first Mexican-American member of the Director's
Guild of America and brother of screen legend Gilbert Roland) puts some muscle into the slicing
of his birthday cake, to the amusement of director Mitchell Leisen and co-stars baby Davy James,
Marlene Dietrich and Fred MacMurray.

Moontide (20th Century-Fox, 1942)
On the set of his ill-fated first Hollywood picture, French film star Jean Gabin watches original
director Fritz Lang (replaced by Archie Mayo) light the candle on a cake as co-stars Ida Lupino
and Mark Hellinger stand by.

Waterloo Bridge (Metro-Goldwyn-Mayer, 1940)
One year after arriving in Hollywood to star in *Gone With the Wind*, Vivien Leigh is presented
with a cake marking the anniversary by her stand-in Mozelle Miller.

Golden Boy (Columbia, 1939)
When the studio wanted to fire William Holden from his first real screen role, Barbara Stanwyck
intervened on his behalf and he became a star. Immensely popular with actors, directors and crews
alike, Miss Stanwyck assists in the cutting of a cake at a party on the set of *Golden Boy*.

Opposite: **Flight for Freedom** (RKO, 1943)
On the set of the fictionalized account of Amelia Earhart's disappearance, star Rosalind Russell
rolls up her sleeves and gets down to the business of serving up some cake.

Following pages: **Saratoga Trunk** (Warner Bros., 1945)
Whoever he was, Frank Campbell's 75th birthday brought out the stars. John Warburton (second
from left), Florence Bates, John Abbott, director Sam Wood, Jerry Austin (front, with cakes), Ingrid
Bergman, Gary Cooper, and Flora Robson turned out to wish Mr. Campbell a happy birthday.

Left: **The Heiress** (Paramount, 1949)
On the set of the film that would
garner her second Academy Award
as Best Actress, Olivia de Havilland
joins director William Wyler in shar-
ing their July 1st birthdays (her 33rd,
his 47th). The annoying Miriam
Hopkins leans into the festivities.

Following pages: **The Major and the
Minor** (Paramount, 1942)
It may be assistant director Oscar
Rudolph's birthday, but director Billy
Wilder seems to be telling him
where to make the appropriate cut in
his birthday cake as co-stars Ray
Milland and Ginger Rogers look on.

Above: **Between Us Girls** (Universal, 1942)
Despite her family name and studio build-up, Diana Barrymore's Hollywood career never took off. While filming her second of only six films, she joins co-star Robert Cummings in assisting producer/director Henry Koster in the cutting of his birthday cake.

Opposite: **Fallen Angel** (20th Century-Fox, 1945)
Upon completion of *Fallen Angel*, Alice Faye, who had been 20th Century-Fox's top star for ten years, walked out on her contract and retired from the screen. Here she slices one of her 33rd birthday cakes under the imperious gaze of director Otto Preminger.

Following pages: **The Wild One** (Columbia, 1953)
On the set of his fifth film, a beefy Marlon Brando watches with hungry anticipation as birthday celebrant-director Laszlo Benedek cuts into his birthday cake. Brando and Benedek are joined by character actor Robert Keith (third from left) and co-star Mary Murphy (next to Benedek), as well as members of the crew.

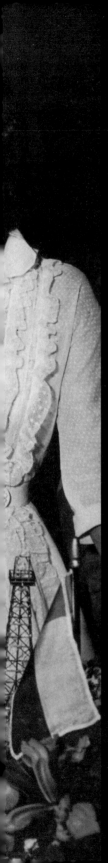

Preceding pages, clockwise from top left:
Three Sailors and a Girl (Warner Bros., 1953)
Jane Powell celebrates her 24th birthday with co-stars Gene Nelson, Jack E.
Leonard and Gordon MacRae. Dance director LeRoy Prinz casts a wary eye on
the proceedings.

Houseboat (Paramount, 1958)
Sophia Loren marks her one-year anniversary in the United States with young
co-stars, Paul Petersen, Charles Herbert, and Mimi Gibson.

The Swan (Metro-Goldwyn-Mayer, 1956)
Six weeks before her engagement to Price Rainier, Grace Kelly was honored
on her 27th birthday on the set of the film in which she portrayed a princess
about to be married. Wishing her good luck are co-stars Brian Aherne, Jessie
Royce Landis, director Charles Vidor, Estelle Winwood, Robert Coote, Alec
Guinness, and Louis Jourdan.

Glory Alley (Metro-Goldwyn-Mayer, 1952)
Leslie Caron brought a cake to work, which made co-star Ralph Meeker
extremely happy.

Left: **Giant** (Warner Bros., 1956)
Film giants James Dean, Rock Hudson, and Elizabeth Taylor pose with a
oil-derricked, flag-festooned cake at a party on the set of George Stevens's
classic film. Dean completed his work November 17, 1955; thirteen days later
he was killed in an automobile accident.

Left: **Forever Darling** (Metro-Goldwyn-Mayer, 1956)
Their real-life marriage foundering, Lucille Ball and
Desi Arnaz began the shooting of their first
independently produced feature film with a wedding
scene. To wish them luck, the crew presented them
with a wedding cake and a doll that wore an exact
replica of Lucy's wedding costume.

Following pages: **To Catch a Thief** (Paramount, 1955)
Director Alfred Hitchcock's 55th birthday is
commemorated by stars Grace Kelly, Cary Grant,
and assembled cast and crew in various stages
of fancy dress.

Above: **The Greatest Show on Earth** (Paramount, 1952)
Hyperkinetic Betty Hutton is presented with a cake on the flying trapeze (she played a trapeze artist in the film) in honor of her 30th birthday. After the film was released, Hutton walked out on her Paramount contract when the studio refused her demand that her second husband, a choreographer, direct her films.

Opposite: **Les Girls** (Metro-Goldwyn-Mayer, 1957)
Hungarian-born ballerina Taina Elg (center) celebrates her 27th birthday with her co-stars, the wonderful Kay Kendall (in her first U.S. film) and the pert Mitzi Gaynor.

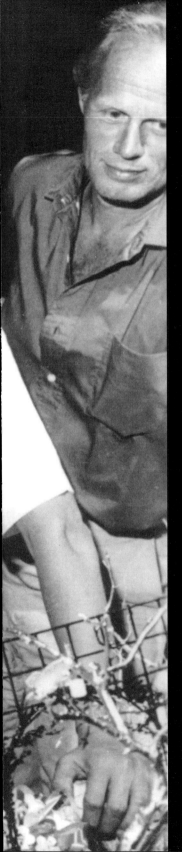

Above: **One-Eyed Jacks** (Paramount, 1961)
On the set of the only film in which he starred, produced, and directed, Marlon Brando observes his 35th birthday with co-star Pina Pellicar, whose tiny cake seems something of an afterthought and may have had something to do with the dour expression on her face.

Left: **The Alamo** (United Artists, 1960)
Under the watchful eye of first-time director John Wayne, fellow cast members Linda Cristal, Frankie Avalon, Laurence Harvey, and Richard Widmark focus their attention on the cutting of a cake.

Opposite: **The Nun's Story** (Warner Bros., 1959)
At the party marking the end of filming, director Fred Zinnemann and star Audrey Hepburn are applauded in honor of their 51st and 29th birthdays.

Following pages, clockwise from top left:
Romeo and Juliet (Paramount, 1968)
On his 17th birthday, Leonard Whiting blows out the candles on his *profitaroli* as director Franco Zeffirelli, actor Milo O'Shea and co-star Olivia Hussey wish him well.

Project X (Paramount, 1968)
Producer, director and schlockmeister supreme, William Castle (*The Tingler*, *13 Ghosts*, *Straight Jacket*) is presented with a cake in honor of his 54th birthday by cast members Christopher George, Greta Baldwin, and Monte Markham.

The Singing Nun (Metro-Goldwyn-Mayer, 1966)
Singer/actress Juanita Moore's 43rd birthday is blessed with the help of Debbie Reynolds and some faux nuns.

Who's Afraid of Virginia Woolf? (Warner Bros., 1966)
Writer Edward Albee wanted James Mason and Bette Davis, but the studio gave him Richard Burton and Elizabeth Taylor. The result was the most successful screen pairing of the celebrated '60s superstars. Here Richard Burton slices his 40th birthday cake as Liz helps herself and Liza Todd waits patiently between them.

Above: **The Birds** (Universal-Alfred Hitchcock, 1963)
Belying his reputation as being aloof with actors ("I did not say actors are like cattle, I said they should be treated like cattle"), Alfred Hitchcock threw a surprise party for actress Veronica Cartwright on her 13th birthday.

Opposite: **Fun in Acapulco** (Paramount, 1963)
The juvenile sidekick was a staple in Elvis Presley films of the 1960s, and Larry Domasin filled that role, helping Elvis's character, a former trapeze artist, conquer his fear of heights in the wake of a tragic circus accident. The King helps Larry celebrate his eighth birthday.

Acknowledgments

In appreciation of their spirit of generosity and encouragement, a heartfelt thank-you goes out to Robert Cushman, Stacey Behlmer, Scott Curtis, Steve Garland, Lynne Kirste, Janet Lorenz, Frans Offermans, Cecelia Sonsini, Danny Woodruff and, especially, Horsefeathers.

All photographs courtesy of the Academy of Motion Picture Arts and Sciences Margaret Herrick Library Center for Motion Picture Study.

Author David Marsh is unable to control himself as his sister, Anne, blows out the candles on her 12th birthday cake. Palo Alto, California, 1958.

About the Author

David Marsh is a native Californian. A writer, he lives under piles of paper ephemera, photographs and artifacts, all detailing cheesy 20th Century popular culture.

Front cover, top to bottom:
Third Finger, Left Hand (Metro-Goldwyn-Mayer, 1940)
William Powell (left) and Melvyn Douglas surprise Myrna Loy on her 35th birthday.

The Story of Dr. Wassell (Paramount, 1944)
Director Cecil B. DeMille celebrates his 62nd birthday on the set of his 66th film.

To Catch a Thief (Paramount, 1955)
Makeup man Harry Ray spoon-feeds Grace Kelly, who is wearing the gown that prompted Alfred Hitchcock to declare, "There's hills in them thar gold."

Front cover, large photo:
Angel (Paramount, 1937)
Director Ernst Lubitsch marks his 25th year in film as Marlene Dietrich looks on.

Back cover, top to bottom:
Pin Up Girl (20th Century-Fox, 1944)
Comedienne Martha Raye enjoys her 27th birthday with pal Joe E. Brown.

How Could You, Jean? (Paramount-Artcraft, 1918)
One of the earliest Hollywood cakes was sent to Mary Pickford in 1918 by an Aussie fan.